Puff the Sea Lion
A Love Story

Puff the Sea Lion
A Love Story

Mary Ellen Ostrander

Sue,
Thank you for loving the
animals.

Mary Ellen
Ostrander
11-8-14

Lewis Sebastian Press
P. O. Box 16952
Rochester, New York 14612

Glory to God,
from whom all blessings flow

CONTENTS

Preface

I have a story to tell. This is how I remember him and I can't wait for you to meet him. There are friends you meet and random experiences you have in life that help you become the person you are. Sometimes these experiences are good things and sometimes not so good. I know love is a wonderful thing. I am a Christian and I believe all that is good is God and that He is love. I believe Jesus came to earth to show us how to love. I love God and He has made me who I am with the good and the bad that has happened in my life, just like the rest of humanity.

I have to start my story by saying it is just that, my story, entirely personal and subjective, with identities and places kept purposely vague. I am a zookeeper. I have loved every animal I have ever cared for, some with a more simple love, but never a lesser love. When you are the caretaker of a human or a non-human animal, over time the bond grows and, if you are willing to go out of your comfort zone, love grows.

I need to tell you about one specific animal, Puff. He meant so much to me that I wrote this story.

Chapter 1
Flounder Alone

Flounder relaxing on the beach

It was about seven years ago, when Flounder, the male California sea lion at our zoo, ended up alone. The last of his zoo family, Ariel, who was born two weeks before Flounder, had just passed away from kidney failure. He had been with a group of four sea lions, his family at our zoo, his entire life. He was born at this zoo and had never been alone.

I clearly remember the day he was born. It was a sunny June morning, 10 a.m. In May of that year, as a precaution, we had lowered the water level of the pool in the sea lion exhibit because we knew our female sea lion, Sealia, who had recently arrived from another zoo, was pregnant and sea lion pups do not swim well as newborns. Sealia was situated on a level of the pool that was usually underwater. Along with some visitors and other zoo staff, I watched her struggle with labor. Sealia had given birth before so we were confident in her mothering abilities. I remember the final push that brought Flounder into this world and recall thinking he was a very big pup when I compared him to Molly's new pup, Ariel. We didn't know the sex of either pup at the time, but, if size was any indicator, my guess was that this pup was a male and the first pup born that summer was a female. It turned out my guess was right.

After the initial moment of excitement faded, I felt a rush of fear. The pup looked blue and was not moving. I had a couple of emergency nets nearby in case Sealia needed our help removing the pup from the water if he happened to slide into the pool. Before I could react, Sealia began to suck on the pup's face and, starting with the nose, broke the membrane that I had failed to notice on the pup. I didn't know it at the time, but all sea lions are born encased in their embryotic sacs. Surprise to me! The membrane slid away and the pup began to vocalize loudly. Immediately, Sealia answered him with her distinctive call and they bonded. Sea lion mothers and pups recognize the unique call from each other whether on the California coast or here at our zoo.

Flounder had a full life at our zoo. He had other sea lions to play and sleep with and his zookeepers loved him and took good care of him. Time went by and, one by one, the others in his family passed away due to old-age related health issues. Flounder was sixteen years old now and I worried about how he would handle the solitude.

It wasn't very long before he started acting differently; for instance, after a feeding he would follow us off his outside beach to our exit doors as if he didn't want us to leave. I mentioned this to my supervisors and they told me they were already looking for a sea lion companion for him. I asked myself, "Until then what can I do to keep him mentally satisfied?" To engage his mind, I purchased a variety of toys to hide fish in. Manipulating a toy to dispense fish is a problem-solving activity that would benefit Flounder physically through exercise and would also stimulate him mentally. He would have opportunities to decide how he would get the fish out of these small holes within the toys. We also added extra training sessions to assure his day remained exciting and upbeat.

Flounder and his kind are very intelligent and easily trained through positive reinforcement. Sea lions can dive 800 feet, deeper that any human diver, and swim up to 25 miles an hour. Did you know that even today sea lions are used in the armed forces in different activities to keep our nation safe? Over the years our country has trained other animals as well. Pigeons were taught to dismantle bombs in World War II. They were trained to pull at the colored wires to dismantle the bomb.

I am very interested in positive reinforcement training. I believe people should treat animals and people with love and respect. Positive reinforcement training is rewarding or reinforcing a specific behavior you would like an animal to do. If you give your dog a treat for sitting, he or she is more likely to do it again. When you are consistently positive with an animal, always kind and gentle, and reward them for being calm and gentle in return, a relationship will grow which is hard to define without using the word *love*. There have been numerous books written about positive reinforcement training and I have read many. Animals do not need someone to control and dominate them, they need someone who will understand and teach them. The communication we humans can have with other species is amazing and life changing.

I was talking to a preacher at a wedding reception recently. This man gave a beautiful sermon during the ceremony about Jesus and love. It was great. We were sitting down for dinner and it just so happened that my mother was at our table. She said, "My daughter trains animals at the zoo."

The preacher said, "Oh, an animal trainer. My wife's father trains horses."

I looked over to his smiling wife who was pregnant and smiled back. I said "That's great. Horses huh?"

He said, "Yes. You should see my father-in-law. He walks right up to the horse and punches him as hard as he can to show the horse who is boss. Then he trains them."

I was speechless. I have spent most of my adult life training sea lions, hyenas, polar bears, orangutans, cattle, spider monkeys, leopards, you name it, and I have never thought of hitting one. I give them treats to reinforce the behavior I want. Before I know it, the animal offers only calm behavior during a training session. The animal becomes relaxed and, to my delight, gentle. But I did not say any of this to the preacher and his wife. What I did say was, "I heard your sermon and I know you believe strongly in Jesus. Jesus would never hit an animal."

The wife folded her arms and looked taken aback, but thoughtful. My father was listening to this brief discussion. He had just recently brought a rescue dog into his home and he was trying to train her by yelling and hitting her with a newspaper. Since that dinner conversation, I have not seen my father use the newspaper. My parents' dog was not socialized. Therefore, she lacked most social skills and jumped up on everyone who entered the house. I taught her to get her toy whenever she became excited; usually it was when I stopped over for a visit. This distracts her and gives me the chance to tell her how good she is.

In closing, I mentioned to the preacher and his wife that it was not necessary to hit animals, or children for that matter. I said, "Try rewarding them for the things you do like." I told them I don't hit my pets or children. It came from my heart. I really meant it. Just reward animals or children whenever they are doing something right. They end up offering that behavior more frequently and the other unwanted behaviors less often. My two children are no different. As they were growing up I would say things to them like, "That was wonderful; you two were talking so nice. Let's go for a bike ride." Or "Let's make cookies." Try it and you will see it works.

Chapter 2
Puff Arrives

Puff (bottom) and Flounder (top) cuddle up together.

But that was not the story I set out to tell. I guess everything is connected. I will share it all. Flounder was a sixteen-year old, male California sea lion, weighed about 420 pounds, and was neutered. In the 1990s there were too many sea lions in captivity and not

18

enough homes for them. Many males were neutered. It was the responsible thing to do. I am not sure if this remains a common practice. Since Flounder was neutered, he could not breed with any of the female sea lions including his mother, who continued to live at our zoo for many years with Flounder. She passed away in her sleep a few years prior to the events of my story at the age of twenty-eight.

After Ariel's death, Flounder realized he was alone and began to show signs that he was not enjoying his life as much as he did when he had company. I had read recently that some animals enjoy the companionship of different species if they are alone, so I started contacting fish hatcheries. I imagined Flounder swimming with a school of fish pushing them left, herding them right. Emulating natural behavior was our goal. After calling a few places (like ten), one great guy called me back with a price. I had to obtain a health certificate, zoo veterinarian approval, supervisor permission, and cash allocation. Finally the live fish, perch and bass, were delivered. The fish were deposited into the sea lion pool and everyone waited to see how Flounder would react to such a natural event. Flounder immediately began to engage with the fish; for over an hour he interacted with them, but he did not eat all of them. I had made sure Flounder was full from his regular meal before I offered him the live fish. Flounder began guiding them around the pool under his flipper. He also carried them in his mouth only to release them unharmed in another area of the pool. He would collect a different fish and deposit it somewhere else. I wondered if this was a natural behavior or if he was just creating games for his own entertainment. Flounder really enjoyed the fish therapy, so we decided to share the live fish with the river otters and polar bears.

Polar bears do not eat fish in the wild; they eat the blubber from seals. We substitute lard for seal blubber and, for variety and enrichment, we add fish to our polar bears' daily zoo diet. Live fish are a special treat we occasionally give them to satisfy their basic need to hunt. Our polar bears worked together hunting the fish—one would corner the fish while the other captured it. All predators need to exercise their hunting instincts, including humans, the top predators on the planet. I shop for bargains—that's hunting for me.

Puff the Sea Lion

My supervisors told me there were no female sea lions available to live with Flounder. They all had homes. Flounder would not live long alone. I just had a feeling about that. I had known him all his life and I did not like the way he was behaving. About six weeks after he started living alone, I was told there was a young male available to be Flounder's companion. Flounder was such a gentle male I thought it was a great idea.

The pup was ten months old, 110 pounds, and his name was Puff. I knew Flounder's life would become a lot fuller now. I was happy. Really, Puff saved Flounder's life. Social animals should be housed with compatible animals if that is how they live naturally. Sea lions live in colonies. Some parts of the year males live in bachelor groups, while during breeding season they will not tolerate other males at times. It is a complex situation.

Puff would have to be quarantined for one month. That is one of the regulations that must be followed whenever a new animal is obtained. I met one of his keepers who accompanied Puff on his trip to our zoo. She looked at his new home and said he was "one lucky sea lion." I never asked her exactly why she said that. She could have noticed the goofy look on my face or the other excited staff members. I could not wait to meet him. I had not worked with a sea lion pup in fifteen years. I had a cake made that read WELCOME PUFF. He was a welcomed addition to our little zoo family. All of Puff's new caregivers and his former trainer shared in the cake while we talked about Puff and his future. Puff received a new home, a new zoo family, and, of course, some fish.

As his first month went by, Puff remained quarantined within the inside poolroom while Flounder stayed outside in the big pool. The quarantine period is necessary to reduce the possibility of transferring an illness (better to be safe than sorry and also because "those are the rules"). It also gave them a chance to get acclimated to each other. Puff was lonely for attention, so I spent all my breaks and lunches talking to him, feeding him, and petting him. He never showed fear. I was falling in love with this one pretty quick. I had never met a wild animal that liked to be petted so much. He needed us. This was new to me and I enjoyed making him happy. I really bonded with him. Trust me, it was easy to do. That month was a long one for both of us.

At last the time had come. Would Flounder accept him? Puff was so small. Puff and Flounder were able to smell each other through some fencing. They started sleeping next to each other, one on either side of a fenced door in the pool area where Puff was being quarantined. With the gate closed between them, they were sleeping next to each other, their most relaxed state. That was a promising sign; it was an indication of acceptance. We sea lion keepers fed them next to each other with the gate shut, but they could see each other. They watched us pet the other saying gentle words. At the end of the quarantine period, we felt they were almost ready to really meet. We brought Flounder inside so Puff could get used to the outside pool by himself. We showed him where he could exit the pool if he felt unsafe. After Puff felt comfortable, Flounder was given access to the pool also.

Flounder chased Puff for a while, but then he stopped and looked up at us. Flounder was watching us for our reaction. Immediately we told him how good he was because he was calm and not chasing Puff.

Flounder wanted a friend and always wanted to please us. We were very fortunate. It's been my experience that when you spend enough time with an animal, you can read each other's body language. I saw Flounder's acceptance of the new arrival in his relaxed swimming patterns and calm facial expression. Flounder understood what we wanted and that's how they began their relationship. Flounder was the boss and Puff just wanted to be near him, next to him, and on top of him. Flounder was so tolerant. They played tag and slept next to each other for the next couple of years.

Puff's other friends were the visitors to the zoo. The exhibit has an underwater viewing area where Puff would engage the staff and visitors in play. The viewing area is inside and heated, so playing with Puff took place all year long, including wintertime. The viewing glass is about thirty feet in length and we raced small toy cars on the window sill for hours. On my break I would start the game with one of my children's cars and Puff would chase it. When my break was over, I would pass the car to a volunteer, docent, or any visitor that wanted to play with the sea lion pup. What an experience for Puff and the visitors, not to mention myself! Our bond grew stronger. Puff could have easily elected to play in a different area of his habitat if he preferred, but he chose to spend his time near people. I believe that because of all this fun and positive interaction with humans, Puff genuinely liked people. He associated all those good times and good feelings with his human friends. When people visited his enclosure he was so excited, but very gentle. I once brought a little girl to the sea lions' inside area to visit Puff. She was in a wheelchair. Puff approached her chair and let her pet him. Right then and there I knew Puff was extremely special. His trust changed me—I became a better person. Watching the connection between a young wild animal and a young person was unforgettable. The experience made me think beyond myself and that moment. The emotional depths of human interactions with animals are just beginning to be appreciated by people.

Puff grew and grew and grew. He learned many behaviors. He kept Flounder young whether Flounder liked it or not. At a certain point, we started seeing little changes in their behavior toward each other. They were barking more. They started displacing each other on the beach. We were now entering into the summer months and June marks the beginning of the breeding season for California sea lions. Their gestation is nearly a year, a three-month delayed implantation and a nine-month pregnancy. At the time we did not have female sea lions. Should they still be exhibiting this natural rutting behavior?

I started doing some research. What do male sea lions do in the wild? What do they do in captivity? I wanted them to have the best quality of life that our zoo could offer. I really cared about these guys, so I started to read more and called other facilities to see how they handled their males during breeding season. What I found out is that every facility handles things differently because of exhibit design and the various ages and sexes of the sea lions in their zoo colonies.

Since Flounder was neutered, Puff would grow to be the larger of the two. I have read that in the wild, the largest male sea lion secures the best real estate on the beach while attracting and keeping the most females. Bigger means stronger, and larger males can fast for longer periods of time because of their higher body weight. Therefore, not only does the largest male retain the best beach with the most females, he can keep it for a longer period of time. If necessary, the fasting can last as long as ninety days. During one of their first summers together, when Puff was small and too young to breed, Flounder fasted for fifty-four days during the breeding season even though there were no female sea lions and he was neutered! He still wanted to be in charge of the beach.

The few facilities I spoke to and visited said that their bigger males were in charge; they were the beach masters. Flounder was 390 pounds and eighteen years old and Puff was 330 pounds and three years old. We decided we had to watch for any signs of aggression beyond simply barking. On the California coast, male sea lions do wound each other during breeding season if one refuses to back down. I have even heard of a male castrating another male who insisted he was the beach master when the other sea lion thought otherwise.

Puff learned a lot from Flounder. Flounder was always gentle with him when he was a pup. I thought Puff had a very good role model. Aggression is learned. So far both sea lions had been compatible with each other and cooperative with us. This remained the case until one day when I came into work and another sea lion keeper said that there was a medication card completed by the zoo veterinarian directing us to put ointment on Puff's wound. I thought, "Wound? What wound?"

Now in retrospect I should not have been surprised, but I, along with many of you, tend to think positively. Either playing got a bit rough or Puff overstepped Flounder's comfort level. I had never put ointment on an animal's open wound, at least not while he was awake. I went out onto the sea lion beach with the other sea lion keeper and we called Puff over to us. He had an eight inch gash on his chest. It was in the blubber and not in the muscle, so I was told it should heal quickly with the antibiotic cream I was to apply to the wound. I felt queasy. I did not want to cause him any pain. It must have hurt. He was ticklish, as his skin was sensitive, like most of us. Our skin is our largest organ, which is true for every other mammal. I have met many animals that have been ticklish, although I have only read about rats being ticklish. In my experience, my dogs and cats, a pair of soft Amur leopards, two sweet mountain lions, two good-natured

Arctic wolves, and, not to forget, two fuzzy hyenas *were* ticklish. So here I was ready to help Puff. I held my breath and put a glob of ointment in the wound and gave him lots of fish. So far, so good. That is how I trained sea lions and still do today—build trust one fish at a time. After applying the ointment twice a day, every day, for about a month, the gash healed.

Would this happen again? Breeding season was just about over and Flounder and Puff were by now the same size. I noticed Flounder riding on Puff's back one day in the inside pool and I thought that was pretty submissive behavior by Flounder, but I only saw it the one time.

Autumn came and Puff learned a lot of new behaviors. He could learn something new in one feeding. He could wave, salute, open his mouth and allow us to touch his teeth and tongue. He let us rub his belly and he would spin around and around. He was a 400-pound puppy. We would play Frisbee for an entire feeding. He was the best retriever I have ever met.

I have two children. When I learned I was to become a mother, I read a lot about brain development in children. I wanted to give them the best possible start in life. I read that children should get unlimited healthy fats until the age of two years old. I also read that the more you read to them and the more things you give them to explore, the more active their brains will become.

My children had many pairs of shoes because there was not a puddle they didn't miss or a mess they couldn't make. (Later they learned to clean up!) That is also part of the adventure of growing up. They are both brilliant young men now. Why am I telling you this? Because when I was raising Puff, I tried the same thing. He showed great intelligence at a very early age. I have read that play is great for brain development. I have also read that animals, people included, will not play if their basic needs are not met. A hungry animal will not play. An animal that is in pain or afraid will not play. Just think of yourself. Do you want to go bowling or play tag if you are really hungry, or you have the flu, or you just got in a car crash? See what I mean?

I observed Puff one afternoon as he was floating a few inches under the water watching snowflakes land on the surface of the pool. His eyes would track where the snowflakes landed and he would tap them with his nose, over and over. "Boink, boink," I said to myself as he touched hundreds of snow flakes, like a child catching them on his tongue. He looked so content and relaxed. To me this indicated that we had succeeded in providing him with a comfortable environment. I felt happy and, in a way, successful that his life seemed carefree and full.

I brought countless toys to the gallery glass for him to see. He liked action/light-up toys, cars, and tennis balls the best. One Valentine's Day I hid a big, shiny foil heart (the lid from a box of chocolates) behind my back. He swam over to the glass waiting for the surprise. He loved the anticipation and so did I. I pulled out the large red aluminum covered valentine. His eyes sparkled and he exhaled thousands of bubbles in surprise. Success! He liked it! I put it behind my back again, ran the length of the glass and he followed along with me. I showed him the Valentine once more and he expelled the bubbles again. What fun! Puff's favorite color was red. He always chose the red toy over any other color no matter what type of toy it was.

When I would go shopping, I always looked for new toy ideas for him. I had to find toys that would not fall to the bottom of the sea lion pool and subsequently enter the filtration system. "No smaller than a football," I was told. One day I gave Flounder and Puff eighteen plastic flower pots. I put a fish in each one, nine were yellow and nine were red, and I hid them on land all around the exhibit. An hour later I came back to see if they had found the pots and pushed them into the water to get out the fish. They had. At the time, Puff did not know how to fetch, so I asked Flounder to clean up the pool by fetching the flower pots. Flounder fetched seven of them and I ran out of fish to use as rewards. I carried the pots away and rinsed them in the sink and set them off to dry. I looked at the seven pots, they were all yellow. Flounder preferred yellow!

Puff's favorite toy when he was very young was a little red traffic cone. Because it was smaller than a football, he could only have it when I was there to supervise him. That little nut would swim right to the intake of the filter and watch as the force of 100,000 gallons of water per hour sucked that cone to the filter grating. He would pull it off and do it again and again.

This got me thinking about other toys he would enjoy. Remember the plastic bowling sets we used to play with as kids? Plastic, buoyant, colorful, a perfect pool toy as long as he wouldn't stick it in the filter intake. So I bought them. I tossed the plastic pins in the pool. He loved them. He tried to hold them underwater with his armpits. (But, of course he didn't have arms...his "flipper pits" we will call them.) I watched as he took them to the filter intake one by one. *This guy wants me to lose my job!* I thought. The aquatic life support staff would be very mad if they found a bowling pin in the million dollar filter system. I watched as he pulled the first pin down with his flipper pit then went to get another and another. Then he would pull one pin off the filter and watch it go to the surface. This game lasted until my lunch was over and I had to get the toys out of the pool. Soon I taught Puff to play fetch so I could get the potentially filter destroying toys out of the pool before I moved on to my other daily duties.

Teaching animals to retrieve new and novel items is a very handy tool to have. I taught our female polar bear and male hyena to "get their toy." The theory behind this is to prevent the animals from ingesting foreign objects that they might encounter. They will give them to the keepers instead. The animal understands after training that the object is worth a fantastic food item in exchange. This is still amazing to me after all these years.

One day I noticed a piece of burlap that used to cover a window in the polar bear holding den. After our female polar bear gave me the usual bucket lids in trade, she looked around for something else to redeem and discovered the burlap and slid it under the door. That was the first time she used the trade game with me for something other than fun and occupation. What a great feeling. An untrained animal may have consumed the burlap and may have become ill. Training saves animal lives—that is a fact.

When I taught the orangutans to trade years ago, I could not pass their exhibit without them pushing "gifts" out to me through any opening in their enclosure. I received sticks, toys, straw, and even poop, for heaven sakes. Very often, when an animal learns a new behavior, he or she is rewarded and praised so much that they offer this new behavior when they have not been asked; it is very cute.

When I taught Flounder to fetch in the early 1990s, he was living with the four members of his family. I will never forget one incident. It happened at the end of the day, of course. They had just eaten their last meal of the day and one of them pooped, so the pool was cloudy.

A man was videotaping the sea lions using a very large camcorder, typical for the 1990s, when the camera's very large battery fell into the sea lion pool. Flounder was only two years old at the time so I knew he would play with that battery all night long. I figured *that* could not be healthy. I could not see the battery, the water was not clear, to say the least. Flounder was the first sea lion I taught to fetch so he was our only hope. I ran back to the diet kitchen and for some reason I grabbed only one fish. Now, there were five sea lions in that pool. What was I thinking? I blame youth and overly positive thinking.

Imagine all the sea lions swimming back and forth barking. The noise was deafening. They always made a lot of noise before they got in a cozy sea lion pile in the evening before they fell asleep for the night. I asked Flounder to swim through the chaos to fetch the battery. He looked at me and dove into the murk and mire of sea lion madness. Didn't he come up with that battery!

The man was waiting for his battery. Was he kidding? I walked into the chaos and called to Flounder with one hand outstretched and holding the bucket containing a single mackerel in the other hand. Through the mayhem he darted passed the other sea lions and handed me the battery! "Good boy!" I said. As I handed him that glorious lone mackerel, the dominant male swam by and snatched it!

Oh! I ran back to the kitchen and got a lot of fish this time. When I returned, I immediately gave Flounder a fish or two and from that point on he has fetched every time I have asked him.

When Puff learned to fetch years later, he added his own retrieving flair. I would come on to their exhibit beach and he would be waiting to give me a stick, leaf or a pinecone. I keep these treasures to this day. I would put them in my pocket and pet him while thanking him for these gifts.

One day when he was very young, I was working with Flounder while Puff was awaiting his turn. When Flounder finished eating, he dove into the water and

Puff quickly jumped in after him and started following Flounder very closely. I stayed to watch to see what was happening. Flounder excreted in the water right where Puff was. I said to myself, "time for me to go." Even for me that was a bit gross. As I was leaving, I saw Puff grab something out of the water and he jumped up to give it to me. It was a quarter. Flounder had defecated pocket change. This must have happened before. Why else would Puff do what he did so deliberately? He thought Flounder was a toy dispenser. Yes, I took the quarter from Puff's proud retrieving lips and yes, I saved it with all my other treasures from Puff.

Now we knew that Flounder was a coin eater. I know some pennies are toxic. No one should eat money, anyway you look at it. From now on, we would have to keep a closer eye on his health. Why do people think they have to throw money into animal enclosures? Don't they know how dangerous it is for the animals? It could kill them. We really love these animals and we need to keep them safe. I determined that the visitors would need to be educated about the harm they may be causing the sea lions and to empower them to stop other visitors from making this terrible decision. I started training Flounder and Puff to allow me to use a metal detector on their bellies. They had to be desensitized to the strange, new "toy." I had to turn the detector on so they could get used to its unfamiliar beeping noise and blinking red lights. Then they needed to accept being touched by the toy. Finally, they had to roll on their backs and allow the strange toy to slide across their stomachs. Both Flounder and Puff learned quickly.

Chapter 3

New Friends

Puff (left) and Flounder (right) snuggling

Environmental enrichment is the part of my job I enjoy the most and training is a part of enrichment. You can see why. I am greatly enriched each and every day in my life because of the animals I care for and I try to return that energy back to them so that I may enrich *their* lives. Cleaning enclosures, maintaining facilities, and diet preparation are among a few of a zookeeper's many duties and they take up a large percentage of the workday. We also engage the public, order food, buy toys, clean glass, bin fish, trim bushes, shovel snow—the list of duties is virtually endless.

In the area where I worked, our team was responsible for a variety of animals. We shared in their care and I personally feel it made it more interesting for the animals to have different caretakers interact with them. During these years, I helped care for two spotted hyenas, two Arctic wolves, two mountain lions, two Amur leopards, two Canada lynx, three Amur tigers, thirty African penguins, two emu, two polar bears, a snowy owl, a salt water coral reef tank, and the two California sea lions, of course.

Three people would share the care of these animals each and every day. We had a lot of work with little time for play, but it is the play time I remember the most. I grew to love each and every one of these animals very much. You *cannot* come in everyday, year after year, when you are sick, when they are sick, when your family is sick, Christmas, Easter, Mother's Day, my birthday, their birthday, snow storms, pelting rain, and the times when it is so hot that just walking is an effort, and not develop an unbreakable bond with the animals that you are there to care for. Our job is to keep them cool in the summer with pools, misters, fans, and shading devices and warm and dry in the winter with shelters, heaters, straw and shavings.

We also devise problem-solving games for them because in the ocean off the California coast, sea lions are continuously solving problems such as avoiding predators, finding and catching fish, choosing a safe beach to rest on. With this in mind, we give them fish hidden toys, hoses to tug on, ice cubes of various sizes to toss around in the water, and squid-flavored "Jell-O-fish" to investigate. They need to have problem-solving games as much as a safe place to live and if we get it right, they will have fun. That has always been my goal; provide fun and good quality of daily life for every animal in my care. Each one of the animals I care for has specific needs, not just because of their species, but because of their individual personalities.

During the Halloween season children dress up and collect candy at the zoo. Puff would be underwater, glued to the gallery glass, so he could follow and chase the little princesses and firefighters. He loved their colorful, sparkly costumes. I caught him trying to look into their goody buckets. I pointed out to the children Puff's interest in their buckets and costumes and the fun continued.

Later that evening, I went to the store and bought him some plastic pumpkins so I could hide fish in them for him. Puff thought that was great and...the pumpkins would not fit in the filter! I heard some children saying one day, "I wonder what color pumpkin Puff will have today?" The families were identifying with him. When people start caring for one animal, they begin respecting an entire species (at least that is what I have noticed). Puff was an ambassador for his species. Because he was so very special, consider with me the 287,000 sea lions in the wild for a moment, each one possessing an individual personality. It's interesting to imagine all those unique beings living in our oceans. It is a lot for me to grasp.

When Christmas arrived, I hung stockings with care. On each one, in glittery letters, sparkled the name of one of the animals I cared for. One day, the staff was hanging Christmas decorations in the gallery where Puff played under water every day. He watched for hours through the viewing glass while the volunteers and staff put up the tree and garland. He especially liked the shiny ornaments. We would roll them back and forth to one another along the window sills and Puff would follow. He never got tired! I had to round up the recruits, the children. My mother had given me a bag of silver and gold-colored plastic ornaments. I would bring one to the glass window and show the children how interested Puff was and the game would begin. Then I would be free to care for the other animals. Now that he had the children to occupy him, I did not have to leave him hanging like that. Otherwise, he would look like a puppet without strings, bobbing in the water waiting and looking for something interesting to do.

Flounder was a good companion, but he wrote off playing not long after his childhood. So I wondered to myself, "When will Puff stop playing with us? I guess when he grows up." I did not want the fun to stop. I noticed families were coming back to the zoo with their own cars and balls and other toys they thought Puff would like. That made me very happy. When I watched

Puff and the visitors playing, I could see by the smiles they were happy too. The visitors were getting a very special treat—a life experience they would always remember. Someone as beautiful as Puff had to be shared.

As Christmas was approaching, Santa and his elves were at the zoo every weekend to visit with the children. Puff floated at the glass watching the human interaction and he was learning. He saw Santa (wearing his big *red* suit) with the children. After the children left, I asked Santa and his elves if they would like to actually meet Flounder and Puff. Santa and the elves had seen Puff floating and watching. They commented on how they watched him observing them and they could not wait to meet him. Off we went to the outside sea lion area.

I grabbed a bucket of fish, and with Santa and the elves by my side, we stepped onto the sea lion beach to visit Puff and Flounder. Puff jumped up on a rock near us. Flounder watched from a distance wondering if it was safe or not. Santa, the elves, and I fed, petted, and praised Puff. We were having a lot of fun. After a few minutes, Flounder wanted to participate too, but he wasn't sure how. He started fetching the toys out of the pool and tossing them to us. And with a little coaxing he was soon next to me and Santa. The elves and Puff completed our circle of laughter and praise. It was a time in my life I will forever cherish. Sea lions and humans enjoying each other, for no other reason than the Christmas spirit and fish!

I realized that every time Puff learned a new behavior our bond grew. Training is a form of communication and relationship building. Puff would participate in play sessions for rubs on the back or head and my telling him how wonderful he was. I loved petting him. A California sea lion's wet coat might look like a rubber inner tube, but it doesn't feel like one. Puff's fur when dry was as soft and fuzzy as a fresh peach and when wet was as smooth as silk. Looking into his eyes, those big chocolate pools, so innocent and trusting, and gazing down at his heart-shaped nose, my heart melted every day. He was growing up to be quite the sea lion. He was gentle and playful. I could not wait to go to work every day. I am serious. I had that Christmas morning feeling *every* morning.

Chapter 4

"The Babies"

Star (left) and Angel (right) sunning
themselves on the beach

One day I was notified that we were adding two female sea lions to our little zoo family. I really felt Flounder had a great life with Puff. They slept together every night. Puff was a snuggler and Flounder, who wasn't, eventually accepted it. Every night they would bark themselves to sleep. They looked like spoons. Puff seemed so happy playing with the visitors at the underwater viewing glass and playing tag with Flounder. We gave them attention, live fish to hunt, and plenty of toys to play with. What else could a sea lion in a zoo want? I remember the last day the males were alone very clearly. I knew a lot would change. I just didn't realize how much.

"The babies" is the nickname we started to call the newcomers. Two female California sea lions, one and a half years old, 110 pounds each, and pretty darn adorable, had arrived. They were both born somewhere on the California coast. They were wild-born, shot by humans, and rehabilitated at a marine mammal center in California. Yes, the marine mammal center's veterinarians removed bullets from these pups! The pups were unable to be returned to the ocean because of their handicaps. One was shot in the right flipper and hobbles on land now. The other was shot in the left eye. Her eye was removed.

I did some research about human and sea lion conflict. Wild sea lions sometimes steal fish from fishermen, so some fishermen respond by shooting at the sea lions. This has been going on for years, as long as there have been guns and sea lions. I know people have to feed their families and I do not have an answer. My heart still breaks when I see the "babies" and contemplate what happens to so many other sea lions.

So here they were, fresh off an airplane and brought to our zoo. Once again, protocol required us to put them in quarantine for a month. We opened a room that had not been used in years, but was built as a sea lion isolation room and has a pool. This I will refer to as the "ISO" room. It sure came in handy. "The babies" would be separated from the males for a month. We had to get to know them and find out what they liked. "The babies" had to feel comfortable and safe with us in order to have a good quality of life.

First we had to name "the babies." For their safety, they had to learn to come when we called them. Since Flounder was named after a fish, and Puff sounded like a shortened form of puffer fish, I reasoned another fish-inspired name would be a good choice. So my son and I came up with Starfish and Angelfish. The staff agreed we should call them Star and Angel for short. We wanted to get them comfortable enough where they would take fish from our hands, but at first we just tossed them fish so they would associate us with food and, hopefully someday, fun. That is how we began our relationship with the babies—with gentleness and fish. I did not know anything about their past circumstances except for what I have told you. They must have been so afraid after being shot, placed in an animal hospital, then put in a crate, then on an airplane, and now here at our zoo. Who knew what their memories were? We had to start giving them good memories. Here we go again! I felt a protective bond growing after just meeting them.

Now I had even less time than ever to spend with Flounder, Puff, and the other animals in my care. I was having a hard time filling their needs. I was overwhelmed, but my anxiety to give them a good life pushed me to a new level. When you have something that is very important to you, you find the strength. I asked God to give me that strength. Some moments were easier than others and I only showed the animals my calm or playful self. None of this was their fault and years ago I chose this job knowing there would be difficult times.

The pups were lucky to have each other, someone to sleep with and play with while they were waiting for the quarantine month to be over. There was a gate within the inside holding area where Flounder, Puff, Angel, and Star could sniff each other. It was so cute to watch. I knew Angel and Star had been with sea lions at the rehabilitation center and in the ocean. Flounder hadn't been near a female sea lion for a few years and Puff, well he didn't know what to think of all this. We laughed at all the sliding around and gentle sniffing. Things were looking good. The staff and I were getting excited as we all knew they would be living together soon. We needed to devise an introduction plan.

We decided to lock the males inside and let Angel and Star acclimate to their new home in the outside pool. Flounder and Puff watched as the babies hydroplaned passed their fenced-in area to explore the large outside pool and rocky beach for the first time since they arrived at our zoo. It was winter and there was ice on the beach. We had given them ice and snow to play with during the time they were quarantined. They were so small that from their perspective they could not see the large pool outside over the rock work.

We tried enticing them with different fish. They had no interest in food. So I decided perhaps snow might lure them outside. Angel led the way hobbling next to me for little snowballs. I continued with encouraging words while pushing snowballs closer and closer to the water. The anticipation was grueling. I thought they would dive in without looking back. They were so inquisitive during their month inside, I imagined them leaving their outside exhibit and sliding rampant through the zoo. No, they just kept sliding in and out of the doorway until one snowball proved exciting enough to follow into the outside pool. We all cheered as Angel and Star explored their new home for the first time like little mermaids in Atlantis. Then, believe it or not, we had to train them to go back inside. They are very good students. They learn so quickly. It was a long journey for them. I was relieved and happy for them, but this was only the beginning of our sea lion introduction plan.

We decided Flounder was the male sea lion the babies should meet first. He had been calm and mostly gentle with Puff. He was raised with a sea lion family in the past. He had sea lion social skills. Flounder was the only sea lion Puff had ever known, unless he remembered his mother back when he was ten months old. So Flounder was it. We separated Flounder from Puff in order to introduce one sea lion at a time. Flounder went outside and immediately dove into the pool. I ran down stairs to the underwater viewing area. I did not want to miss a thing. Several staff members were on the beach to observe and help the pups if needed.

I will never forget what I saw. I never read this in any book, journal, or paper. Flounder ignored them and floated on the bottom of the pool quietly. He did not look at them. Angel and Star approached him underwater, darting this way and that. Since their arrival, I had not seen their true ability to swim— amazing, graceful, and now purposeful. The more I watched, the more it reminded me of the dog behavior books I had read. A dog that is well socialized does not run up to a dog he doesn't know. He looks down or around, moves slowly and acts calm to show the other dog his intentions are not aggressive, but peaceful. Flounder had planted himself on the bottom of the pool looking away from the babies and started to scratch himself with the nails he has on his rear flippers. He had not done this before. He grooms himself out of the water. It was so obvious to me he was trying to make them feel relaxed and comfortable. I was so proud of him. All my anxieties went out the window. Flounder would be a fair ruler of our new little charges.

Eventually the babies did calm down. They appeared to be sniffing him under water; all was still and slow as they continued to get to know each other. Soon they started to swim together. Star and Angel would porpoise—leaping out of the water quickly and gracefully—on occasion to stretch the flippers that had to be less active inside during their month of quarantine. This part of the multi-step introduction process went well—just a few grey hairs added to my head. Now it was Puff's turn. How was the biggest pup in the zoo going to react to this well balanced and serene new family unit?

Well, I will tell you what he did. He came bounding out like a 450-pound puppy. He glanced around the beach. You could see it in his eyes; he looked relieved—good the coast is clear—and then he dove right in. When he saw Star and Angel with Flounder, he got out of that pool so fast, climbed to the highest rock, and gave another look. I was laughing inside at his blatant disbelief of the circumstances. Then he dove back into the water and hovered behind Flounder, who was now a bit smaller than he, seeking comfort. Flounder let Puff stay with him providing emotional stability for the group.

Star was the first to approach Puff. Puff did not act relaxed like Flounder. No, he swam away as fast as he could, but he was no match for these little mermaids. The chase was on and Star was gaining on him. When Puff turned to look at her I saw he was getting an erection. As I was thinking *"OH BOY!"* that one-eyed sea lion pup, Star, bit Puff's almost erection and Puff came to a dead stop. Then he lay on the bottom of the pool and became very still. From that moment on Star was in charge of Puff. Where she learned that survival technique, we will never know—perhaps in the wild or at the marine mammal center. Maybe it is instinctual and not learned. It may have saved her life in the wild. Today, it made her dominant over a very excited, large male pup, who obviously was lacking in the social skills department. I was glad Star took charge. She had a disability, so this turn of events would make this very new family more balanced.

Chapter 5

The Rivals

Flounder (right) secures prime real estate on the beach
from Puff (left) during a breeding season.

Not long after this initial introduction, Puff
started following Flounder again, but with a different
intention. It did not look like it was for comfort
anymore, but for control over the pool. He was
following right behind Flounder with an intense look in
his eye. Just a short while ago he was next to Flounder

looking meek and sheepish. How quickly these animals were changing their behavior; it was hard to keep up. I was rooting for the peaceful leadership of Flounder. I guess everyone was hoping they would be one big happy family. Optimism is a very useful tool to have. So that was our goal.

In reality, we had a very large sea lion pup living with female sea lions for the first time. He also had few sea lion social skills and was obviously entering his first rut out of season. On the other hand, we had an older, neutered male who, of course, had less testosterone, weight, and stamina. We were still hoping that based on Flounder and Puff's relationship, along with Flounder's life experience, that Flounder would continue as the dominant male. Well, we were wrong.

It did not take long for the males to start swimming faster and faster, Puff's bulk behind Flounder. Flounder would turn opened-mouthed towards Puff, but that did not change Puff's quest one bit. Soon Flounder was out of the pool heading inside with Puff on his tail. Flounder went into a corner and ignored Puff's barking and lunging. I could see it in Flounder's eyes, the fight was over.

Why didn't Puff see what I saw? Now what? Once you separate animals, it is very hard to reintroduce them later on, especially in our situation where the female sea lions were a permanent part of our family now.

What I read later is that aggression is learned. If it is allowed to continue, it escalates. In the training books I have read, they stated that the worst case scenario of unchecked aggression is death. The best thing is for aggression never to start. Humans behave this way also. Just say, for example, your dog is doing something you don't want him to do, and you yell at him, but he does not stop. You may use a newspaper and swat him, but he still doesn't stop. In theory the punishment will escalate and you'll use your hand and if the dog still doesn't stop, then you may resort to a more harmful weapon. Eventually, the weapon will get more dangerous until the dog is destroyed. Instead, reward your dog for what you do want—observe him, then praise him or give him a treat for behaving the way you want. You will shape the behavior you desire.

Puff had quickly learned to be aggressive toward Flounder; we never expected such a quick change. Puff could not unlearn this aggression so we decided to train him to an alternate behavior. If Puff was engaged in this alternate behavior, he couldn't corner Flounder. I wasn't sure we could change the outcome because the struggle for dominance is a natural male sea lion behavior, but you never know. When Puff came into the inside holding area (which was where Flounder fled to get away from Puff) to dominate Flounder, we would ask Puff to lie down before the aggression started. We really wanted them to get along. It was difficult to watch. We thought we could fix anything with positive reinforcement training. After many fish, what we ended up with at the end of the day was Flounder still in the corner of the holding room, looking away, obviously not happy, and Puff lying flat in the middle of the room staring at the keeper door waiting for his next fish. Well, it was a start, but there was only so much time we could work with him; we had to take care of many other animals and we had to go home sometime.

Then, of course, the aggressive behavior would resume. In the wild, the submissive male would be able to move on. Flounder tried to go farther and farther away. I found him hiding behind their collection of toys one day and in the ISO room another day. He was submitting, but Puff didn't understand. However, Puff would lie inside staring at the staff door for hours waiting for a fish, not bothering Flounder. This was the best we could do.

It wasn't good enough. Flounder was getting tired and Puff was relentless. Puff, who I believed saved Flounder from a life of loneliness, was now Flounder's rival. It was a natural behavior we were dealing with. We had to help Flounder regain his quality of life. We decided to separate the males. They would each have half a day living with the females outside and the other half staying alone in the inside pool area. The outside animals had the option to come in and visit the inside animal. This took a lot of time and effort, tons of planning, and a great deal of fish!

First we had to train each male to enter the ISO room alone. They had to enjoy this room. They needed to look forward to entering this room anytime we asked which would be several times a day. We needed to make it fun for them. Countless times I brought Flounder or Puff into this small room, fed him, and played games with him.

Puff the Sea Lion

At first they were leery. Sea lions are prey animals. Killer whales and great white sharks hunt and eat them. I have noticed that prey animals are a lot more cautious than predators, for obvious reasons. They had to trust me. I had to reinforce it, making it fun over and over again. I made sure they did not feel forced or tricked. It became a game they wanted to play repeatedly. Not long after training began, I would find Flounder or Puff waiting for me in the ISO room looking forward to a fish or play session. Every chance I had, I played the game with them and they started to anticipate it. Soon I was closing the door of the small ISO room and reinforcing that. It is truly wonderful to be part of a trusting relationship like this. Flounder and Puff humbled me with the honor. With Flounder and Puff's new locked-in behavior, they could take turns going in and out any time of the day. For their keepers, it was a very powerful tool to have at our disposal to help enrich their lives.

Chapter 6
It Takes a Village to Raise
a Sea Lion

Conducting a training session with a bucket of fish for each with
Flounder (rear) and a young Puff (front)

With Starfish and Angelfish's arrival we needed
to add personnel to the sea lion staff. Our new charges
had no training whatsoever. They were wild sea lions.
We needed to teach them many husbandry behaviors

including being separated from each other. To my knowledge, they depended greatly on each other, so we had to gently get them accustomed to being alone for a short time. In the past on my scheduled work days, I worked alone with the sea lions. Now the sea lions were in need of more people to care for them. The only problem was that the only other person in the zoo besides me who had actually taught behaviors to these sea lions was leaving the zoo to work elsewhere. We had a few people who had done some animal training in the past, but all weren't familiar with positive reinforcement training. In other words, we had staffing issues. I realized I now had to teach staff how to train sea lions that had never been trained before, which created additional concerns. For a while it was a challenge. One thing was for certain, however, our staff was dedicated.

Their devotion was heartwarming to observe. At times, there would be a problem. For instance, Puff would come when he was called; this should not have been a problem, this is what he was supposed to do. But to a person who had not worked with a sea lion of Puff's size (500 pounds), or with his speed (because he was so young and enthusiastic), or a person who had never worked with sea lions before or had not trained an animal before, Puff could seem intimidating. Therefore, he was intimidating to them. I did not want the sea lions to be afraid and now I had to make sure the new trainers did not fear the sea lions and enjoyed their time with them. I couldn't always be there and I knew the sea lions would get better care if the staff looked forward to the time they spent with them.

Seven different zookeepers were caring for four sea lions; most of them were new to the sea lion world and three of the sea lions were new to our world. If you figure out mathematically how many different animal/keeper scenario mixes that occurred each day, let alone in a week, give me a call. I know it was a lot to adjust to, but I'm happy that we pulled together and gave them a great life. We had to be consistent for the animals' sake and also for our own.

Helping to care for the sea lions, seeing their raw beauty and innocence, turned these co-workers into very good friends of mine. We were on a pilgrimage, a quest to give these animals an excellent foundation for the rest of their lives. We wanted them to know only kindness and gentleness. We weren't the top trainers of the country and we did disagree at times, but we pulled together. Each of the sea lions was taught to be separated at any time, to be alone in any room without fear along with many other husbandry behaviors.

Chapter 7

Fun and Games

Treasures I keep.

When Puff was with the females they engaged in a lot of play, especially the game of "tag." This is my favorite story about Star and Puff. We used a wooden door stop to hold a door open to one of the holding rooms. Although the sea lions had an abundance of toys, I would often find that door stop missing. Puff would dash outside and get it for me whenever I asked him. He was so good. One day as I was walking by the underwater viewing windows, I saw Star zipping through the water with that door stop in her mouth. Puff was hot on her heels. He knew it was not for her. She had the prize among prizes and he would never be able to catch that little imp. They were enjoying each other and having the time of their lives, at least Star was. Puff looked on with hopelessness in his eyes. He could not stop chasing her as fast as he could. She had always been too much for him to handle and now—the doorstop! Poor guy—he could not get enough of her.

The aquatic life-support staff, who are in charge of all the pumps and motors that make the pools function, would lose their eyes if they saw that potential filter-destroying object in the pool. After watching for another minute, I knew I had to act quickly. I went to the diet kitchen, armed myself with a dozen mackerel, (every training battle needs a weapon), and set off to the sea lion beach. I needed that door stop. I was giggling inside. Star didn't know how to fetch yet, so Puff was my only hope, but he was hopeless when it came to Star.

When I entered the outside beach area, I saw a sea lion game of keep-away in progress. Puff had the doorstop behind him floating in the water. He didn't dare turn to grab it because Star was bobbing in front of him waiting for him to make any false move. This was high stakes, intense fun. I knew the feeling when I was a child. I really didn't like it when my brother would take my things and run off with them. Now here I was again, confronting that same problem from a different perspective.

I went to the edge of the pool armed with the bucket of mackerel. Puff was bobbing there in this sea lion standoff. "Fetch Puffy," I said. He turned quickly to look at the doorstop. I said, "That's right, good boy." Star dove for the doorstop, but Puff blocked her assault. Then Star, as quick as the wind, was next to me trying to find a land route to confiscate the beloved doorstop. At that moment Puff dropped it by my feet; I snatched it up a second before Star and put it in my fish bucket for safe keeping. I gave Puff a dream's worth of mackerel. The playful imp and her friend, Angelfish, received a few fish—just because. That was fun! "I really have to get a chain to hold that door open," I thought as I left those little nuts. As I passed the underwater viewing area, I peeked at them to see if they were forlorn without the doorstop. I saw Star swimming at top speed once again, Puff on her tail, and a leaf in Star's lips.

Their fun would not stop, with or without the doorstop. How could I not love them?

When Flounder was out with Star and Angel, calm ruled the land. If Star was sassy, Flounder's presence quieted her. They would be beached together in the sun even though Flounder protested. He still was not a cuddler. They liked each other and swam together, relaxed and confident. Where Puff *needed* to be near the females, the females *wanted* to be near Flounder. Isn't that just like life?

Angelfish, quiet and beautiful with her little lame flipper, would come inside later to rest with them or play quietly alone when the others were resting. It was good to see her independent from Star. Angel was starting to feel at home. I was glad for that. The quiet ones are noticed less because they need a different kind of attention.

Chapter 8

Puppy Love

Star resting behind Puff

Breeding season was about to begin. I had concerns about the females becoming pregnant at two years old and giving birth at three years old. Although impregnation was possible, they would not be physically mature until eight years old and to tell you the truth, I didn't know if Star would ever be mentally mature (ha ha!). Heaven only knew if Puff was ready to share space with another pup or two. I had to get some facts about young sea lion mothers.

Male sea lions bulk up before breeding season. This allows them to fast for months and focus on breeding while freeing them of the inconvenience of having to hunt and eat. Would both males fast and refuse to switch places on exhibit when we ask them to? They both equally enjoyed the females' company in their own way. The females' lives were enriched by the time they spent with each male. What was going to happen in the next months? I would have to get all our sea lion staff on board with all the facts about sea lion breeding and the males' change in demeanor during rut. Males can beach for up to one hundred days and may become territorial during their rut. I had to worry about how Puff would act with our new staff and how the new staff would handle a rutting male sea lion for the first time. We had to make educated choices because we might not be able to depend on Puff's trained behaviors. He would have other things on his mind.

Were the females too young to breed? I read that the females showed the males they were interested in breeding. Their vulvas turn pink and they would ride on the males' backs. I also read that copulation could occur on land or in water. Years ago I had worked with an intact male living with receptive females. His name was Nemo. I only recall observing actual copulation once. So I wondered if it would be obvious to our staff. Our current sea lions were so young. What was to happen?

Puff grew again until he reached 515 pounds. Although he was still eating, he ate less. He thought Star was the universe. I saw her vulva pink only one day. Puff slept all day when he was locked inside. Yes, he left his females during rut. Not because of food, but, to our surprise, to rest. Those babies were exhausting him at night. Thank God.

Flounder had his time with the females too. He even started fasting, despite being neutered, but he would still come into the inside holding room or go out to the beach when we asked. We did have some tough moments, however. One time I asked Star to come in so I could get a very busy and barking Puff to come inside too. Star didn't seem to mind being Puff's bait. What a good sport. Then Flounder would go outside and all would be calm and Puff would go to sleep.

I noticed all of our training abilities had increased as a team and as individuals. We were now thinking on our feet. The entire staff was skillfully acting as one with safety as our top priority.

Then we started discussing re-introducing the males to each other. We decided to keep the females out of the mix, at least initially. This meant we had to train the females to go into the ISO room during the time we had the males together. Every day around noon we locked the females in.

We reasoned that if Flounder was given access to the outside pool and beach before Puff, that it might establish Flounder's dominance. We did not want Flounder to be chased at all knowing Puff's aggression would only escalate if allowed. We decided to have a controlled feeding: Flounder stationed at one area and Puff at another, Flounder facing Puff and Puff's back to Flounder. I was nervous, but we had to give it a chance. They used to be constant companions and they still slept next to each other with a gate closed between them. They had the freedom to sleep anywhere, yet they chose to be next to each other.

I was in charge of keeping Puff stationed and interested in me. Another trainer kept Flounder stationed and focused near her. Our plan was to reintroduce them gradually, just a minute the first day, then adding a minute each day until they were comfortable with each other again. It was necessary to start with small increments; we wanted success.

Flounder was already outside with his trainer when I brought Puff out. Puff looked at Flounder and Flounder looked at Puff. Puff was just inches away from me. I said his name. He broke eye contact with Flounder and looked at me. I gave him so many fish he could barely swallow them and then he followed me around the exhibit. I was so excited. We would do this one fish at a time. Puff would peek at Flounder, but then look at me...more fish.

Then Flounder's trainer moved Flounder towards the inside. I wanted them to move faster. I didn't know how long Puff would find the fish more enticing than chasing Flounder. When Puff turned to see what Flounder was up to and saw he was gone, he left me so fast to see where Flounder had gone, it made my head spin. I was so glad Flounder was inside and they displayed no aggression towards each other. I called Puff back to me and, when he was stationed and calm, his reward was "the babies". The females came out and they started to play, chasing each other around, swimming about, and making lots of noise. Now I needed to get Puff back inside so Flounder could finish his time outside and it worked. Occasionally, it took a little time, but it was all worth it. They found the activity stimulating and so did the staff. Our relationship continued to grow with the sea lions, trusting that all experiences would be positive and good ones. We made sure they were.

Staffing patterns changed; our days off from work interfered with the training. The reintroduction was moving very slowly, but it was all safe and promising. During one training session in particular, Flounder broke station and swam right over to Puff. I thought this showed Flounder was getting comfortable with the situation. This had to be a good sign. Then Flounder's trainer got his attention again and brought him inside before any harm was done. Another close call! These two were destined to be the end of me, but I loved every minute because every minute we were trying to improve their lives.

Chapter 9

What's wrong with Puff?

Puff resting on the beach.

Unexpectedly, we had to bring the reintroduction program to an end, at least for a while. Puff had a swollen jaw. His jaw felt warm when I touched it. We guessed it was either a bruise or an infection. I had to train him to keep his body still and put his face on an x-ray plate so we could see what was going on. We spent most of our training time and a lot of fish to get Puff used to having his jaw manipulated, even when it was painful. He was just getting accustomed to all of this, when the vet staff asked us to teach him to accept an injection instead. I said, "Sure" and the training changed course. It is necessary at times while training to adjust your thought patterns to benefit the animal.

Puff wasn't the first animal I had to train to receive an injection. When I started injection training the animals in my care during these years, I purchased twenty wooden back scratchers to desensitize the Canada lynx, Amur leopards, spotted hyena, Amur tigers, mountain lions, and polar bears to being touched. I gave them their favorite food treat while touching them with the back scratcher so they would associate the feeling of being touched with a delicious treat. To this day all twenty back scratchers are intact. This amazed me at the time, but not anymore. Only one animal turned to grab the back scratcher because he wasn't eating at the time (my fault, of course). It was the male hyena, but that is a different story.

I taught Puff to present his tail to us and let us approach him and hold a syringe to his back end. All this new training took time, so in the interim, the vets prescribed oral antibiotics for Puff. After a week of training Puff, I told the vets that Puff was ready to be hand injected for tranquilization. Then I realized I could not reward him with fish for taking the injection. He could not eat before he was tranquilized—he might aspirate. Instead, I would have to use praise to reward him.

In addition, Puff would have to be trained to be locked away from all water. If he dove into the water for comfort and safety while he was under anesthesia, he could drown. His jaw wasn't getting any better with the antibiotics. I trained Puff to come in from the outside, go into a pool, and let Flounder go outside. Then I would bring Puff into a water-free environment to receive the injection, which was the most difficult part of the training process because he was uncomfortable when he was locked away from water.

Since the vet staff wanted to treat him without delay, it was decided that Puff would receive his medicine using a tranquilizer gun instead. I felt disappointed because we had spent so much time working on this procedure which I believed could have been stress-free for him. I wanted to do what was best for Puff and knew this immediate intervention could save his life. I would make it up to him. I told him we would have so much fun when he woke up.

The next morning Puff and I began learning this new routine to prepare him for the dart. He was a quick learner. Reinforced with a blend of praise and fish, he was fearless and soon ready for his procedure. I notified the vet staff; they were ready to go as well.

The next day Puff came inside as usual. When I opened the door to the waterless room, he slid inside, all without food!

The vet took one step inside the waterless room, aimed, and fired the dart. Twenty minutes later Puff was lying still, staring at the pool he had been locked away from. However, he was not asleep. I walked in to retrieve the dart. Puff was so still. The vet staff checked the dart. The medicine had not discharged from it. It was a misfire. Poor Puff. We had worked so hard, but he was not going to be treated that day.

Why was he so still? I went in and opened the pool for him. He slid in and rested in the water quietly. I think Puff didn't know what to make of the strange man who came out from behind the door and the loud noise of the dart gun. I went into the kitchen and grabbed a bucket of fish. I had a relationship to work on and possibly to mend. We started playing the games he enjoyed: fetching, sliding room-to-room, and spinning around and around. All the while I was praising him. He was slow at first to participate, but within ten minutes, he was back to his old self. I was very proud of him. He trusted me so much. His innocence was so shiny, it dazzled me.

Just fifteen minutes later, I walked to the vet office and told the vet staff he was ready again. They were going to figure out what happened with the darting mechanism. We would try again in a week's time. I was happy to have more time to rebuild any trust I might have lost with Puff.

The following week, Puff did not falter, thank God. The entire procedure went like clockwork. He was tranquilized and his tooth was removed. The vets gave him a good dose of antibiotics and returned him to his water-free holding area to recover. The vet and I stayed with him well into the evening to watch for any problems. I hoped this was the end to any health issues for him. He was wonderful and only deserved happiness.

For his safety, we decided to wait until the next morning and allowed him time to recover before we provided him access to the water. He was so quiet when I came in and saw him the next morning. He was just lying there. I prayed, "Dear God, please help this poor guy." I slid the pool door aside and Puff gratefully slid into the inside pool. He never thought to bark at me or act aggressive at all. He never categorized me as a danger. He looked at me with relief, when you would think he would be agitated with pain and fear. Our bond became stronger. When I sit back and take this all in, I am humbled once again. How did I deserve such an honor and how could I thank God?

Puff didn't eat for a few days and his jaw bled. When I weighed him he had lost fifty pounds again. Then when he started eating, *he really started eating*, thirty to forty pounds of fish a day and we played games and he learned new behaviors. He was feeling good and so was I. I was very grateful.

Chapter 10

A Stronger Bond

Petting Puff

Now that Puff was on the mend, we had new concerns—specifically the possible births of California sea lion pups.

I immediately began reading marine mammal journals, looking at websites, and talking to different sea lion caregivers from around the country. Once again I found out that each situation is different. I learned young new mothers may have issues nursing their young. So I started training Star to allow me to manipulate her nipples in case I had to train her to nurse her pup. I learned pups cannot swim well right away, so we made a big floating raft for the outside pool.

I mentally assessed the possibilities. I concentrated on making my relationship with Puff as strong as possible. If we had to deal with very protective new sea lion mothers, I needed this large young bull to come to me and be locked away. There could very well be pups diverting the attention of the adult sea lions from their established routines, compounded by the fact that we would have Puff's raging hormones to deal with due to the females being receptive to breeding within a month after giving birth. Plus, there could be pups swimming here and there, not coming when I called them because they would be drinking mother's milk not eating fish. In other words, chaos!

Fish would not be as important to the males as it is most of the year. I would have to find other things that they would enjoy and look forward to; therefore, I made their days very entertaining. I had a great time thinking of ways to surprise them with new training games, toys, and surprise live fish. If this worked, I was hopeful we could maintain their excellent life quality throughout the entire breeding season. It would take a lot of effort and teamwork, but they were worth it!

I was not working the day when Puff's rut began, but one of my co-workers told me his genitals were visible and he began fasting and beaching himself. I wasn't sure what was in store for me the next day, but I was optimistic. When I came to work that morning, the first thing I did was check on the sea lions as I did every morning to assess their health. Puff was acting quieter than usual and there was a large amount of vomited fish on the sea lion beach with coins in it. I could not tell which sea lion vomited, because each of the female sea lions eat fifteen pounds or more of fish a day, but Puff was the one acting "off." Why would someone throw money in their pool? I had taught Puff to fetch so he wouldn't ingest foreign bodies. He had given me coins before. That was before the babies arrived and maybe it was a game Star and Puff played together. All I knew is that he was not feeling well and I could not tell if it was because of the pennies or the seasonal rut. Only time would tell.

I researched the toxicity of coins. I found out that beginning in 1982, pennies are now made with copper plating and a core of potentially toxic zinc, which can cause kidney failure and damage red blood cells. For a dog, zinc poisoning can occur from eating a single penny. Therefore, I told the educators who spoke at the zoo's summer sea lion demonstrations of our plight. They were more than willing to explain to the visitors what we were doing and why. Some people couldn't believe sea lions could get sick from a penny or two, others couldn't believe someone would throw money into an animal's enclosure, and still others couldn't have cared less and just wanted to see the sea lions do "tricks." All I wanted was for the sea lions to be healthy, happy, and playful and to have a good life.

During the day Puff started to perk up and eat. I had found four pennies and a quarter in the vomit. Hopefully, these were the only coins Puff had consumed (if it was indeed Puff who had ingested them). The next day when I came into work I was going to ask the aquatic life support staff if they had recently noticed any coins or vomit in the filtration system. More importantly, I would check on the animals to see how their night went.

What I found that morning in the sea lion holding room I will never forget. There was blood sprayed all over the doorway where Puff, Star, and Angel could go in and out during the night. Flounder was safe in the holding pool, so I knew it wasn't his blood. I was thinking, "What does rut, coins, vomit, and blood have to do with one another?" Or were they all separate issues? I radioed my supervisor who notified the vet staff. Puff looked miserable again. He was not barking. He had been a barking machine ever since the babies arrived. And what was wrong with his mouth? The silence was deafening and once again, I was very worried. Where was the blood coming from? Who was bleeding? Puff would not participate in his usual daily training session, so I could not examine him. Normally, I closely examined him three times a day. I knew something wasn't right. We monitored where each sea lion slept and came to the conclusion it was Puff; he was bleeding from his nose.

For six days Puff would not eat or bark and would not come inside when I called him. The vet staff decided to dart him with pain medication to help him through this. He could not be tranquilized because, as I said earlier, he could fall asleep in the water and we would not be able to get him out. He would drown. If the animals won't or can't come to us, the injection procedure may fail. However, I think that injection training, whether the injection is given successfully or not, creates a bond that is not easily broken. I was really concerned and determined to get him through this.

Most animals mask their pain. Since Puff was showing his discomfort I knew he was not well. The vet darted Puff with pain medication and by the middle of the day, he was swimming around and looking better. Now, our priority was to get Puff to come inside, so Flounder could get his time with Angel and Star.

Puff started to take an interest in Star two hours after receiving the pain medicine. Since Puff wasn't hungry and because neither one found me as interesting as they did each other, I decided to ask Star to come inside to see if Puff would follow her. After partaking in a few shenanigans, Star came in with Puff hot on her heels. Even when sick, he liked her more than fish; she was so important to him. I closed them inside. First I let Star go outside, then Flounder. I then took a deep breath and concentrated on Puff. How could I help him?

Puff's appetite increased that very day and the vet prescribed a daily dose of pain medication for him, since he had improved after the initial medicated dart. We started playing games; as I assessed his health we played an exuberant game of fetch and toss-the-toys-in-the-tub-and-spin-around. If he was enjoying the games and playing with his usual vigor and eagerness, he *had* to be feeling better, right? I didn't know what to think. His nose had stopped bleeding. I weighed him the next day and found he had again lost fifty pounds that week. Well, whatever the reason, he was on the mend. He was back to eating thirty to forty pounds of fish a day and playing with Star and me.

In the next month, Puff gained back the weight he had lost, but he started sneezing. His breath still smelled of the seasonal rut and he was very active pursuing Star. When male California sea lions are in rut, their breath has a turpentine smell to it. I am not sure why. It must be hormone-related though. The year before, his genitals were conspicuous for about a month and he would sleep all day when he was locked in and Flounder was out. His behavior was different from last year. In addition, I did not see his genitals and he was resting more. He was just six years old; some sea lions live as long as thirty years, so chances were his rut would be different from year to year as he and the females matured.

Then his behavior changed; he began to rub his face along the floor, he left training sessions before they were over, and there was another foul odor mixed with the turpentine smell of his breath. Because of his distracted behavior and the odor of his breath, the sneezing was diagnosed as an infection. The zoo vet prescribed an oral antibiotic for him. That antibiotic didn't agree with him and he lay inside holding his belly until he vomited up ten pounds of fish. That poor guy, he couldn't catch a break. Puff was given a different antibiotic. This antibiotic did agree with him and after about a week, I would hear him sneeze only once a day.

What a summer this had become. I had been observing Star and Angel for any signs they were ready to breed. Star had the pinkish vulva last year. This year I think I saw it once. Hmm... If she was receptive to breeding last year, she should be ready to breed this year. What was going on? My time with the sea lions was limited to about an hour a day. One minute here, five minutes there. I have many other duties and several other animals to care for. During my observations and our frequent games, training sessions, and feedings, what was I missing, if anything? I asked the night guard if she had seen any breeding at night. She had not.

After a few days Puff started sneezing again. The vet put him back on the antibiotics. The sneezing stopped. After his third round of antibiotics, the vet decided to tranquilize him again to get a closer look; he would use an endoscope to examine his sinus cavities. I had been working on hand injecting him. Our vet, who is my friend, said he would rather Puff be in a squeeze cage in case Puff turned and tried to bite me. I didn't think that Puff would, since he *never* tried before. We adjusted the training immediately. I needed a second person to help me. Puff was eight feet long. I couldn't be near his back end and his face at the same time because the squeeze cage does not allow the animal within it to turn. The vet staff wanted a good look at him, sooner rather than later, so they decided to dart him again. I just wanted him better. His health had been in question long enough. I felt I could give him the injection, but I didn't want to hurt him.

Once again, he was locked away from the other sea lions and from any water source. Puff knew something was up because when the vet walked in Puff moaned. It broke my heart. He was scared, but he didn't do anything but lie down and accept the vet darting him. I vowed at that moment I would never let that happen again. He was so brave and non-threatening. All animals, including humans, have a freeze, flight or fight response. If we can't get away, we are wired to be still, leave, or defend ourselves. Puff never thought of attacking the vet to save himself, instead he froze, remaining motionless.

Instead of crying in frustration, I got determined. Puff needed me to teach him something new which I was afraid of, but now ready to consider because of the love I had for him.

We waited twenty minutes and Puff still wasn't fully asleep. For some reason the tranquilizing medication did not work completely. Puff was only half asleep. The vet staff entered the room with Puff to supplement the drug to make him sleep. Puff roared at them. I had never heard that vocalization before. (I always thought they should be called sea dogs instead of sea lions because they bark more than they roar). They gave him the medicine pretty easily because Puff was having a hard time moving.

Twenty minutes later Puff was sleepier than before, but he had fallen into this semi-conscious state in front of the only door by which the vet staff could exit. After the vet checked Puff's awareness, he determined that this medicine did not work for Puff. He was still too awake for the exam and the treatment he needed. The vet staff was pretty much stuck in the room with Puff, because Puff's sedated body was blocking the double doors to the inside pool room.

Puff was trying to look around, so I knelt by those doors and started talking to him and scratching his neck through the door grating. Since the procedure was called off, I assumed I could comfort him now. I could tell Puff liked seeing me because he exhaled and relaxed. Whatever medication he received had left him aware, just not mobile. I had trained him to move away and leave doorways before I entered a room. This behavior helped the new trainers feel more comfortable around him because he was big and very eager. Before I opened a door, I would ask him to "go," then reward him when he went to a different room. I told the vet staff this was my plan. I would ask him to leave the doorway so they could exit. They looked skeptical because of his medicated state, but I was hopeful. There Puff lay sedated. I grabbed the door handle and said "go." He looked at me and I said, "Go, Puffy." Didn't he roll away from the door a couple of feet? He couldn't slide away like usual, but he knew what to do! What a good boy. The vet staff exited safely. I loved him even more after that. To this day, the trust he showed me takes my breath away.

I knew he would do it. He would do everything I ever asked of him. He humbled me again. I told him he was a very good boy. The vet staff gave him a reversal drug and he was up and around in a couple of hours eating, playing, and chasing those babies. The vet was going to look into using a different tranquilizer for Puff. We planned on another exam the following week.

Puff began to sneeze more frequently and the smell of his breath was changing once again. We knew that the infection was back. Puff acted like he was in pain. He would vocalize and leave training sessions. The vets prescribed antibiotics and pain relievers and I intensified the injection training. With the medications he was on, I could approach him and train him. Treatment was imperative. With the help of my fellow keepers, I felt I was ready to hand inject him in the squeeze cage. He was sick, but at every feeding he would go into his squeeze cage and get a fake injection. We made it part of his daily routine, no questions asked. I gave Puff the injection and my co-worker then gave him a fish. During training he would get thirty to forty pounds of fish for this behavior.

On the day he was scheduled to be tranquilized, Puff would not be able to eat because he might aspirate due to the medication. A week after the last tranquilization attempt, I believed he was ready for us to try again. Was I ready? I prayed for hours on end to be brave for him, to be strong, and not to hurt him. I would not forgive myself if he looked at me with those big brown eyes and I saw pain or fear. I would just crumple and die. So I prayed and prayed for God's guidance and strength. I emailed sea lion trainer friends of mine at other facilities and they were more than happy to send me papers they had written on sea lion injections. After reading them over, I felt confident we were on the right path.

Chapter 11

The Power of Love

An underwater Puff smiling at me

The morning of the procedure, October 4, 2012, arrived and I was very anxious. My family and friends were all praying for me. I have been through a lot of difficult things in my life, just like a lot of you have. I knew it had to work out, right?

I met with the vet staff and showed them the papers I had from the sea lion trainers I knew. The vet said he would be administering the same medication they used to anesthetize Puff, which made me feel relieved because of this medication's success. Then he said he would like to use the dart gun to deliver the medication. I told him Puff and I had been practicing with the hand injecting in the squeeze cage just as the vet said he preferred. He thought about it and decided we could try the hand injecting.

I hoped Puff was feeling up to it because I was a wreck. I wanted to do this for Puff. I needed him to feel comfortable and not to be afraid. It would be just he and I playing a game. The vet mentioned there was a possibility Puff had a tumor or something else seriously wrong with him. I was sure it was a stick or some other foreign body up his nose like a bee. I was positive that whatever was bothering Puff would be flushed out and it would be games as usual tomorrow.

We had a team meeting. We went over the plan for injecting Puff out of water. Normally, Puff went through this series of behaviors flawlessly. It was October and he was not in rut or preoccupied with breeding. But he was acting "off" again, distracted. With positive reinforcement training the animal does not have to *do* anything; they choose to partake or not and we always reward them with food when they choose to participate. However, today we had to keep him interested in the training and comfortable so he would participate, but fish would not be part of the session. We had never done this before. Puff had always received a lot of fish for everything he did.

I was ready. The team was with me. I wanted this to be a game of going from room to room like before, just a bit different this time. Puff didn't feel well and we needed to help him. The vet came to the sea lion area and said we needed to use a larger needle to get through Puff's blubber and to administer the medication quickly. I looked at the needle; it was much longer and thicker than the one we practiced with. We used a 20 gauge for practice. This needle was a 14 gauge. I thought "Dear Lord help me. I cannot do this alone. Please give me strength for Puff's sake." I held the needle and got dizzy. I loved Puff so much I knew I *had* to do this.

I walked into the room with Puff. First, I had to lock him out of the pools without rewarding him with fish. I put on my happy face and used my play voice. After this was all over, he and I were going to play so much and he was going to eat so much fish his head would spin.

I COULD NOT WAIT for this to be over! He did as I asked and was wondering where the fish was. Next he had to go into the squeeze cage. We would not lock him in it. He would just get his injection there. I gave the bucket of fish to another sea lion trainer so I could administer the injection by his tail. He could not eat, but he needed to do what we asked.

He looked at me as if to say "Mary Ellen, you haven't given me a fish for any of the games we played this morning. Why should I go in the squeeze cage?" And I thought, "Because I love you so very much. Please do as I ask."

The other trainer showed him a big fish on the other side of the squeeze cage. Before his illness, Puff routinely entered the squeeze cage without seeing a fish, but he just wasn't himself. He looked at me. He looked at the open door where the ISO room pool was. I knew he wanted to flee. We left that door open to the ISO pool room for the moments it would take to give him the injection because he would feel most comfortable believing he had access to water. We hoped it would be a few short moments. I had never been so desperate to have something happen before in my life. I said to Puff, "Come on, big buddy, you can do it!"

Puff slid into that squeeze cage so fast, I never got the ISO pool room door shut, but I did give him the SHOT! It happened so fast and so accurately that I know it was in God's hands.

The other trainer said, "I don't know if this is going to work."

And I said, "It already has."

She said, "What? "

And I said, "He got the shot!!!!"

Puff looked at me with the big smile on my face, my arms raised in the air which I do when I can't control myself when he is a very good boy. Then I yelled, "GOOD BOY PUFFY! YOU ARE A VERY GOOD BOY!"

My prayers were answered. I didn't see fear or pain in his eyes; I saw confusion. "Where are the fish?"...then he slid into the ISO pool.

OOPS! I ran passed him to get to the basement to drain that pool. He cannot drown! It drains in five minutes. I was running. I ran passed the vet, the vet staff, and the curator saying, "He got the shot, he didn't feel it. I have to drain the pool. Be back in a minute."

I opened the drain and ran back to see if he had left the ISO pool and he had. He was quietly lying down similar to the previous tranquilizing attempts, staring at the closed pool room door, willing it to open. He felt so comfortable in that pool room.

We left him alone and quiet so the medication could take effect. Then we celebrated with each other by hugging and laughing. This was the first time in our zoo's history that one of our sea lions was hand injected for tranquilization. We had hit another milestone and we were really happy! I personally knew God was with me and Puff every second. I felt weak and He needed me to be strong for Puff's sake and I was. WE DID IT! That was one of the happiest moments in my life.

Twenty minutes went by and the medicine was working. He needed to have gas along with this type of medicine, so the vet staff put a cone on his face while he breathed in the medicine to keep him sedated. Next Puff needed a tube to go down his wind pipe to give him a steady supply of air. He fought this part, so the vets knew he required more gas. I watched and what comforted me was the thought that he would be healthy soon. It was only one day. It would be all right.

When he struggled to get the tube out of his mouth, I will never forget how I wasn't sure what to do. I had absolutely no knowledge of what was needed medically, so I just started talking to him. Although I was eight feet away, he calmed down immediately. Again, it hit me that he means so much to me, but also I meant so much to him. I sometimes wonder how I was given this gift. I felt unworthy. So I talked sweetly to him. The vet gave Puff more medicine and he relaxed. Then we carried him to a truck in a cargo net and took him to the animal hospital for a full exam.

Puff was with the vet staff for a couple of hours. I watched the examination for a while. I was nervous, but I had the other sea lions to care for. They kept my hands and mind busy. I was called on the work radio and notified that Puff was on his way back to the sea lion holding area and they asked me to get ready for his arrival. I prepared the pools and had a humongous bucket of fish waiting for him. I had a lot of making up to do.

Puff arrived sound asleep. We carried him in a cargo net and laid him gently on the floor. The vet staff was getting his vitals before they gave Puff the reversal medication to help him wake up. I stayed out of the way and just watched. I was anxious for this to be over.

The vet staff was working quietly, but I noticed something wrong in the way they were looking at each other. I have known these people for years. I said, "Dear God, please..." But, I didn't know what to ask for. Since Puff hadn't taken a breath in a very long time, I prayed for my sanity (because for the first time in my life I really thought my mind was folding for good). Puff was not waking up. Sea lions have a dive reflex where they can hold their breath for approximately twenty minutes. I had a feeling this was not the case because it looked like the vets were initiating resuscitation attempts.

They started working faster, giving more shots. One vet started massaging Puff's chest.

They said Puff was dead and they weren't sure what happened, so I crawled to him. On my hands and knees, I crawled into the crowd of people and wiggled his flipper and wiggled his tail. He was still warm. I started crying and I am crying now as I write this. I crawled to his head and touched his teeth and his eyes. I pulled the tube out of his throat and I heard his last breath. I kissed his head and I said, "Please wake up Puffy and everything will be okay."

I am not sure how long we were there. It didn't seem long enough. I will never forget the horrible feeling of loss. The vet staff wanted to necropsy Puff to find out why he died. We had never lost a sea lion from anesthesia and we needed to know what happened. We all sat around Puff on the floor of the sea lion holding room crying and petting him. There must have been ten of us there. We loved him very much. Puff was put back in the cargo net and carried back to the truck—a vision I will take to my grave. He would be examined thoroughly at the animal hospital to find the cause of his death.

I watched him being carried away. He's eyes not looking at me for the first time—just blank. I don't know how to describe the pain I felt. My chest hurt so bad I wanted to rip it open to release the pain. I would never wish that sadness on anyone. I knelt down and put my head on the wall and cried and cried. I have never felt such loss. I had never become this close to an animal. I have never had a person depend on me as much as Puff had except for my own children. He was so young and so good.

Chapter 12
God and Grief

My garden

I didn't run from God at this time. I ran to Him as fast as I could. I couldn't talk. I could just pray. Not once did I question God and His choices. I will always be on His side.

I am not sure how much time went by. I remember hugging people and crying. I remember petting Flounder, Angel, and Star knowing they were feeling the loss too. I really don't remember the next few months after Puff's death. I went to work and cried all the time. I spent a lot of time alone. I cried at home. I cried in the car. I cried at the store and in church. I saw Puff at church and in the store. He would just appear. My mind would not let him go.

I went to the library and borrowed books on grief. I went on-line and researched more. I know there is a process in healing after a loss. I read about so many losses and in a strange way this comforted me. I looked in cars at stop lights and wondered if these people have ever felt the way I felt or were maybe feeling it now. Then I started praying for them and for all the people who suffer from such a loss. Will they find God or will they just crumble and perish? Will they lose themselves or will they become closer to God and be who He wants them to be?

Then I went in my back yard and started digging and digging. In the pouring rain I planted hundreds of flower bulbs: tulips, daffodils, hyacinths and gladiolas. Hundreds of flowers and thousands of tears along with memories and fevered prayers were planted that day.

One day I was talking to my oldest son and I just started crying. Up to this point in their lives, my children had never seen me cry. I am usually a light spirit and we laugh a lot in our house. I told him I was sorry and crying helps me heal. He said he understood and he understood that Puff was my animal child—from the mouths of babes. I did not realize that what I was feeling was exactly that. Puff was my animal child and he never got to grow up. I felt better that my family understood. Death has taken pets, grandparents, friends, and other close relatives. Each loss was acutely felt, but I always reasoned it was their time. I guess deep inside I didn't believe it was Puff's time.

What comforts me to this day is that he is with God. He is swimming and playing with God. I see him playing Frisbee with Jesus. Puff was the best aquatic Frisbee player. He never tired of it; imagine a 500-pound puppy in a huge pool. We had so much fun! In my mind it became clear. I believe we all start in heaven, human and non-human animals. I truly believe God has a plan for us; we only have to choose which path to take. I will always choose love no matter where it takes me because that choice I will never regret. Puff had taught me to love beyond the limits I had created. God had given me Puff to learn to love deeper and I have. I thank God every day for the time I had with Puff. I love God more than I ever have.

Epilogue

Training Starfish (left), P. J. Butterfish (right),
and Angelfish (back) on the beach

Just five months after Puff died, Flounder passed away February 26, 2013 from kidney failure. He was twenty-one years old and he had been showing signs he was slowing down—preferring certain fish, sleeping more, losing weight. Star and Angel wanted to sit next to him more, even when it appeared he didn't want company. He would bark and tell them he wanted to lie there alone. Star would not take that for an answer. She would slide closer and closer to him. He would keep barking "No!" but he was tired and she needed to comfort him. After an hour of this, they would be resting together. Then Angel would arrive in her quiet way and Star would bark at her and tell her to leave. What a crew!

After all the barking and protesting, I would find them all resting with each other. Star and Angel are good girls. Flounder was lucky to have them and they were lucky to have him. Flounder was so patient with Puff, Angel and Star. He taught them by example how to act like well-mannered sea lions. He helped so many of us, the keeper staff, by teaching us so gently how to be sea lion trainers. There will never be another one like Flounder. We saw he was very quiet one day. I told him I loved him. The next day we found him dead. Star and Angel stayed with him to the very end. What beautiful animals.

In the necropsy, the vet staff found crushed bones in Puff's nose and a massive infection. That is why he had the nose bleeds on May 31, 2012. That crushed bone had no blood flow through it. The antibiotics could not work. We will never know what he was doing that night when he broke his nose. But I have an idea.

Exactly one year later, June 1, 2013, Starfish gave birth to a little pup. (As I mentioned before, a California sea lion's gestation is one year.) Yes, Puff and Star were breeding that day. I can see him in my mind chasing her in and out the way he always did. Then she would just turn and look at him and he would stop and go the other way and she would chase him. When I think about that—a 180-pound sea lion chasing a 515-pound sea lion, it makes me smile. They always had so much fun together. She was always in charge. Perhaps Puff wasn't looking where he was going during this game of tag and injured himself. The blood I found all over the pool room was from Puff's broken nose.

Puff and Star's pup is a male and we named him P. J. Butterfish. Silly, I know, but Puff Junior would be too painful to say every day. P. J. is half Starfish too. That is where the Butterfish comes in. But, I don't need any reminder. Puff is in my heart always.

Star is an excellent mother. I have watched her teach P. J. to swim, to hide in caves, to listen to each very different call from the first hour he was born—all natural behaviors. Does Star remember when she was less than a year old with her own mother in the wild or is it instinct?

Angelfish plays with the pup and watches Star's mothering skills. Angel has quietly slid in between me and the pup when Star has not been close by. I believe she was protecting him. I am so glad they have each other. There are so many things we do not know about the animal kingdom, but are discovering more daily when we just pay attention.

If you could only see my backyard in the spring and summer now; the bulbs I planted after Puff died bloomed for the first time when P. J. was born. The gardens are an array of colors and the scent is fresh and new. The flowers will continue to multiply and bloom year after year and I'll still cry because I'll still miss him so. I was lucky to have Puff. It wasn't until a year after his death that I realized the depth of our bond; he was in rut and some males will not respond to their trainers during breeding season; he had a broken nose and many animals act aggressive when they are in pain; and he was suffering from a massive infection that was traveling to his brain. He was in *a lot* of pain and still he trusted me.

I don't know what the future holds for me, Star, Angel, and P. J. I really don't want to know. What I do know is that there will be a lot of love and a lot of fun. I love you God. Thank You.

Note from the Author

P. J., our delightful little surprise!

Now that you have read my story, I hope Flounder and Puff will always be alive inside each of you. Thank you for reading it. Many of you may not have realized how much zoo animals can be loved. Now you know. I am not the only person out there who has loved an animal this much. All Creation should be loved.

I could not have written my story without the devotion and editorial skills of Maureen Whalen.

Maureen, besides being the most thorough editor, is a docent at the zoo where I work. She felt the loss of Puff and Flounder with me and relived the good times and bad with me while editing this story and it was not easy....thanks Maureen!

Thanks to my husband, Steve, and my brother, John Blazynski, for their editorial insights and contributions to refining my story. Thanks also to my mother, Darylann Blazynski, and Pamela O'Sullivan for reading an early draft of the manuscript.

Thank you to my husband, Steve, and my sons, Tom and Tim, for being there when I need you most. I love you guys!

I made a new friend designing the book cover. Thank you to Jenelle Penders of Jenelle Lynn Graphic Design for such a beautiful book cover. The picture on the cover is how I remember Puff, gentle and eager to please.

A special hats–off thank you to Sandy Smith for being a guardian angel to me and to so many animals. Most of the photographs in this book are her handiwork and I appreciate her compassion and friendship more than I can convey.

Speaking of friends, I need to thank my right-hand woman, most dedicated volunteer, and Godliest woman I have ever met, a true follower of Jesus Christ, Sherrie Provenzano.

Thank you to all the docents, volunteers, and zoo visitors who played with Puff, the sea lion pup, at the gallery glass. You made a difference in his life. A special thank you to all my coworkers for loving the animals, especially the people who loved Puff and Flounder with me.

Proceeds from the sale of this book will help rehabilitate wild sea lions at various marine mammal centers in the United States. I want the love I had for Puff and the love he had for me benefit wild sea lions. It is my hope that good will come from Puff's unexpected death. It was a marine mammal rescue center that saved Star and Angel's lives.

A portion will also go to Sandy Smith's not-for-profit pet spay and neuter program which has benefited so many animals.

Be sure to visit my website, puffthesealion.com, or you can email me at lewissebastianpress@gmail.com.

About the Author

Mary Ellen Ostrander began working with zoo animals in 1985. She has been married for twenty-five years, has two wonderful sons, three dogs, a cat, and three birds. She is a member of the International Marine Animal Trainers' Association (IMATA), the American Association of Zoo Keepers (AAZK), and the Animal Behavior Management Alliance (ABMA).